CAMPING
JOURNAL

NAME: _____

PHONE: _____

Campground:	Dates:

Location: _Old Man River_____
Travel to Campground: *Miles:*_____ *Time:*_____ *Cost:*_____
Weather/Temperature: _____

Campground Information

Name: _____
Address: _____
Phone: _____
Site#: _____ Site for next time: _____
Cost: _____ $ ☐ Day ☐ Week ☐ Month
GPS: _____
Rating: ★☆☆☆☆☆☆☆☆☆
Water pressure ★☆☆☆☆ Location ★☆☆☆☆
Cleanliness ★☆☆☆☆ Site size ★☆☆☆☆
Restrooms ★☆☆☆☆ Noise ★☆☆☆☆

Amenities:
☐ easy access ☐ back-in ☐ pull-through
☐ water ☐ pet friendly ☐ laundry
☐ paved ☐ sewer ☐ electricity
☐ 15 amp ☐ 30 amp ☐ 50 amp
☐ shade ☐ pool ☐ restrooms
☐ store ☐ picnic table ☐ fire ring
☐ firewood ☐ tv ☐ wifi
☐ security ☐ ice ☐ cafe

Activities:
☐ fishing ☐ hiking ☐ canoeing
☐ lake ☐ river ☐ hot tub
☐ fitness ☐ bike ☐ boat
☐ shuffleboard ☐ pickleball ☐ golf

Camped with: _____
_____
_____

People met: _____
_____

New friends: _____
_____

Places visited: _____
_____
_____

Visit/do next time: _____
_____
_____

Most memorable event:_____
_____
_____

Most fun things:_____
_____
_____
_____

Notes:_____
_____
_____
_____
_____
_____

Drawing or favorite photo:

Campground: _____ Dates: _____

Location: _____
Travel to Campground: *Miles:* _____ *Time:* _____ *Cost:* _____
Weather/Temperature: _____

Campground Information

Name: _____
Address: _____
Phone: _____
Site#: _____ Site for next time: _____
Cost: _____ $ ☐ Day ☐ Week ☐ Month
GPS: _____
Rating: ★☆☆☆☆☆☆☆
Water pressure ★☆☆☆☆ Location ★☆☆☆☆
Cleanliness ★☆☆☆☆ Site size ★☆☆☆☆
Restrooms ★☆☆☆☆ Noise ★☆☆☆☆

Amenities:
☐ easy access ☐ back-in ☐ pull-through
☐ water ☐ pet friendly ☐ laundry
☐ paved ☐ sewer ☐ electricity
☐ 15 amp ☐ 30 amp ☐ 50 amp
☐ shade ☐ pool ☐ restrooms
☐ store ☐ picnic table ☐ fire ring
☐ firewood ☐ tv ☐ wifi
☐ security ☐ ice ☐ cafe

Activities:
☐ fishing ☐ hiking ☐ canoeing
☐ lake ☐ river ☐ hot tub
☐ fitness ☐ bike ☐ boat
☐ shuffleboard ☐ pickleball ☐ golf

Camped with: _____
_____
_____

People met: _____
_____

New friends: _____
_____

Places visited: _____
_____
_____

Visit/do next time: _____
_____
_____

Most memorable event:_____
_____
_____

Most fun things:_____
_____
_____
_____
_____

Notes:_____
_____
_____
_____
_____
_____

Drawing or favorite photo:

Campground: _____ **Dates:** _____

Location: _____

Travel to Campground: *Miles:*_____ *Time:*_____ *Cost:*_____

Weather/Temperature: _____

Campground Information

Name: _____

Address: _____

Phone: _____

Site#: _____ Site for next time: _____

Cost: _____ $ ☐ Day ☐ Week ☐ Month

GPS: _____

Rating: ★☆☆☆☆☆☆☆☆☆

Water pressure ★☆☆☆☆ Location ★☆☆☆☆
Cleanliness ★☆☆☆☆ Site size ★☆☆☆☆
Restrooms ★☆☆☆☆ Noise ★☆☆☆☆

Amenities:
- ☐ easy access ☐ back-in ☐ pull-through
- ☐ water ☐ pet friendly ☐ laundry
- ☐ paved ☐ sewer ☐ electricity
- ☐ 15 amp ☐ 30 amp ☐ 50 amp
- ☐ shade ☐ pool ☐ restrooms
- ☐ store ☐ picnic table ☐ fire ring
- ☐ firewood ☐ tv ☐ wifi
- ☐ security ☐ ice ☐ cafe

Activities:
- ☐ fishing ☐ hiking ☐ canoeing
- ☐ lake ☐ river ☐ hot tub
- ☐ fitness ☐ bike ☐ boat
- ☐ shuffleboard ☐ pickleball ☐ golf

Camped with: _____
_____
_____

People met: _____
_____

New friends: _____
_____

Places visited: _____
_____
_____

Visit/do next time: _____
_____
_____

Most memorable event:_____
_____
_____

Most fun things:_____
_____
_____
_____

Notes:_____
_____
_____
_____
_____
_____

Drawing or favorite photo:

Campground: _____ **Dates:** _____

Location: _____
Travel to Campground: *Miles:* _____ *Time:* _____ *Cost:* _____
Weather/Temperature: _____

Campground Information

Name: _____
Address: _____
Phone: _____
Site#: _____ Site for next time: _____
Cost: _____ $ ☐ Day ☐ Week ☐ Month
GPS: _____
Rating: ★☆☆☆☆☆☆☆☆☆
Water pressure ★☆☆☆☆ Location ★☆☆☆☆
Cleanliness   ★☆☆☆☆ Site size ★☆☆☆☆
Restrooms   ★☆☆☆☆ Noise   ★☆☆☆☆

Amenities:
☐ easy access   ☐ back-in   ☐ pull-through
☐ water   ☐ pet friendly   ☐ laundry
☐ paved   ☐ sewer   ☐ electricity
☐ 15 amp   ☐ 30 amp   ☐ 50 amp
☐ shade   ☐ pool   ☐ restrooms
☐ store   ☐ picnic table   ☐ fire ring
☐ firewood   ☐ tv   ☐ wifi
☐ security   ☐ ice   ☐ cafe

Activities:
☐ fishing   ☐ hiking   ☐ canoeing
☐ lake   ☐ river   ☐ hot tub
☐ fitness   ☐ bike   ☐ boat
☐ shuffleboard   ☐ pickleball   ☐ golf

Camped with: _____
_____
_____

People met: _____
_____

New friends: _____
_____

Places visited: _____
_____
_____

Visit/do next time: _____
_____
_____

Most memorable event: _____
_____
_____

Most fun things: _____
_____
_____
_____

Notes: _____
_____
_____
_____
_____

Drawing or favorite photo:

Campground: _____ **Dates:** _____

Location: _____
Travel to Campground: *Miles:* _____ *Time:* _____ *Cost:* _____
Weather/Temperature: _____

Campground Information

Name: _____
Address: _____
Phone: _____
Site#: _____ Site for next time: _____
Cost: _____ $ ☐ Day ☐ Week ☐ Month
GPS: _____
Rating: ★☆☆☆☆☆☆☆☆☆
Water pressure ★☆☆☆☆ Location ★☆☆☆☆
Cleanliness ★☆☆☆☆ Site size ★☆☆☆☆
Restrooms ★☆☆☆☆ Noise ★☆☆☆☆

Amenities:
☐ easy access ☐ back-in ☐ pull-through
☐ water ☐ pet friendly ☐ laundry
☐ paved ☐ sewer ☐ electricity
☐ 15 amp ☐ 30 amp ☐ 50 amp
☐ shade ☐ pool ☐ restrooms
☐ store ☐ picnic table ☐ fire ring
☐ firewood ☐ tv ☐ wifi
☐ security ☐ ice ☐ cafe

Activities:
☐ fishing ☐ hiking ☐ canoeing
☐ lake ☐ river ☐ hot tub
☐ fitness ☐ bike ☐ boat
☐ shuffleboard ☐ pickleball ☐ golf

Camped with: _____
_____
_____

People met: _____
_____

New friends: _____
_____

Places visited: _____
_____
_____

Visit/do next time: _____
_____
_____

Most memorable event:_____
_____
_____

Most fun things:_____
_____
_____
_____
_____

Notes:_____
_____
_____
_____
_____
_____

Drawing or favorite photo:

Campground: _____ Dates: _____

Location: _____
Travel to Campground: *Miles:* _____ *Time:* _____ *Cost:* _____
Weather/Temperature: _____

Campground Information

Name: _____
Address: _____
Phone: _____
Site#: _____ Site for next time: _____
Cost: _____ $ ☐ Day ☐ Week ☐ Month
GPS: _____
Rating: ★☆☆☆☆☆☆☆☆☆
Water pressure ★☆☆☆☆ Location ★☆☆☆☆
Cleanliness ★☆☆☆☆ Site size ★☆☆☆☆
Restrooms ★☆☆☆☆ Noise ★☆☆☆☆

Amenities:
☐ easy access ☐ back-in ☐ pull-through
☐ water ☐ pet friendly ☐ laundry
☐ paved ☐ sewer ☐ electricity
☐ 15 amp ☐ 30 amp ☐ 50 amp
☐ shade ☐ pool ☐ restrooms
☐ store ☐ picnic table ☐ fire ring
☐ firewood ☐ tv ☐ wifi
☐ security ☐ ice ☐ cafe

Activities:
☐ fishing ☐ hiking ☐ canoeing
☐ lake ☐ river ☐ hot tub
☐ fitness ☐ bike ☐ boat
☐ shuffleboard ☐ pickleball ☐ golf

Camped with: _____
_____
_____

People met: _____
_____

New friends: _____
_____

Places visited: _____
_____
_____

Visit/do next time: _____
_____
_____

Most memorable event:_____
_____
_____

Most fun things:_____
_____
_____
_____
_____

Notes:_____
_____
_____
_____
_____
_____

Drawing or favorite photo:

Campground: _____   Dates: _____

Location: _____
Travel to Campground: *Miles:* _____ *Time:* _____ *Cost:* _____
Weather/Temperature: _____

Campground Information

Name: _____
Address: _____
Phone: _____
Site#: _____ Site for next time: _____
Cost: _____ $ ☐ Day ☐ Week ☐ Month
GPS: _____
Rating: ★☆☆☆☆☆☆☆☆☆
Water pressure ★☆☆☆☆ Location ★☆☆☆☆
Cleanliness ★☆☆☆☆ Site size ★☆☆☆☆
Restrooms ★☆☆☆☆ Noise ★☆☆☆☆

Amenities:
- ☐ easy access   ☐ back-in   ☐ pull-through
- ☐ water   ☐ pet friendly   ☐ laundry
- ☐ paved   ☐ sewer   ☐ electricity
- ☐ 15 amp   ☐ 30 amp   ☐ 50 amp
- ☐ shade   ☐ pool   ☐ restrooms
- ☐ store   ☐ picnic table   ☐ fire ring
- ☐ firewood   ☐ tv   ☐ wifi
- ☐ security   ☐ ice   ☐ cafe

Activities:
- ☐ fishing   ☐ hiking   ☐ canoeing
- ☐ lake   ☐ river   ☐ hot tub
- ☐ fitness   ☐ bike   ☐ boat
- ☐ shuffleboard ☐ pickleball   ☐ golf

Camped with: _____
_____
_____

People met: _____
_____

New friends: _____
_____

Places visited: _____
_____
_____

Visit/do next time: _____
_____
_____

Most memorable event: _____
_____
_____

Most fun things: _____
_____
_____
_____

Notes: _____
_____
_____
_____
_____
_____

Drawing or favorite photo:

Campground: _____ **Dates:** _____

Location: _____
Travel to Campground: *Miles:* _____ *Time:* _____ *Cost:* _____
Weather/Temperature: _____

Campground Information

Name: _____
Address: _____
Phone: _____
Site#: _____ Site for next time: _____
Cost: _____ $ ☐ Day ☐ Week ☐ Month
GPS: _____
Rating: ★☆☆☆☆☆☆☆☆☆
Water pressure ★☆☆☆☆ Location ★☆☆☆☆
Cleanliness ★☆☆☆☆ Site size ★☆☆☆☆
Restrooms ★☆☆☆☆ Noise ★☆☆☆☆

Amenities:
☐ easy access ☐ back-in ☐ pull-through
☐ water ☐ pet friendly ☐ laundry
☐ paved ☐ sewer ☐ electricity
☐ 15 amp ☐ 30 amp ☐ 50 amp
☐ shade ☐ pool ☐ restrooms
☐ store ☐ picnic table ☐ fire ring
☐ firewood ☐ tv ☐ wifi
☐ security ☐ ice ☐ cafe

Activities:
☐ fishing ☐ hiking ☐ canoeing
☐ lake ☐ river ☐ hot tub
☐ fitness ☐ bike ☐ boat
☐ shuffleboard ☐ pickleball ☐ golf

Camped with: _____
_____
_____

People met: _____
_____

New friends: _____
_____

Places visited: _____
_____
_____

Visit/do next time: _____
_____
_____

Most memorable event:_____
_____
_____

Most fun things:_____
_____
_____
_____

Notes:_____
_____
_____
_____
_____
_____

Drawing or favorite photo:

Campground: _____ **Dates:** _____

Location: _____
Travel to Campground: *Miles:* _____ *Time:* _____ *Cost:* _____
Weather/Temperature: _____

Campground Information

Name: _____
Address: _____
Phone: _____
Site#: _____ Site for next time: _____
Cost: _____ $ ☐ Day ☐ Week ☐ Month
GPS: _____
Rating: ★☆☆☆☆☆☆☆☆☆
Water pressure ★☆☆☆☆ Location ★☆☆☆☆
Cleanliness ★☆☆☆☆ Site size ★☆☆☆☆
Restrooms ★☆☆☆☆ Noise ★☆☆☆☆

Amenities:
☐ easy access ☐ back-in ☐ pull-through
☐ water ☐ pet friendly ☐ laundry
☐ paved ☐ sewer ☐ electricity
☐ 15 amp ☐ 30 amp ☐ 50 amp
☐ shade ☐ pool ☐ restrooms
☐ store ☐ picnic table ☐ fire ring
☐ firewood ☐ tv ☐ wifi
☐ security ☐ ice ☐ cafe

Activities:
☐ fishing ☐ hiking ☐ canoeing
☐ lake ☐ river ☐ hot tub
☐ fitness ☐ bike ☐ boat
☐ shuffleboard ☐ pickleball ☐ golf

Camped with: _____
_____
_____

People met: _____
_____

New friends: _____
_____

Places visited: _____
_____
_____

Visit/do next time: _____
_____
_____

Most memorable event:_____
_____
_____

Most fun things:_____
_____
_____
_____

Notes:_____
_____
_____
_____
_____
_____

Drawing or favorite photo:

Campground: _____ **Dates:** _____

Location:_____
Travel to Campground: *Miles:*_____ *Time:*_____ *Cost:*_____
Weather/Temperature:_____

Campground Information

Name:_____

Address:_____

Phone:_____

Site#:_____ Site for next time:_____

Cost:_____ $ ☐ Day ☐ Week ☐ Month

GPS:_____

Rating: ★☆☆☆☆☆☆☆☆☆

Water pressure ★☆☆☆☆ Location ★☆☆☆☆

Cleanliness   ★☆☆☆☆ Site size ★☆☆☆☆

Restrooms   ★☆☆☆☆ Noise   ★☆☆☆☆

Amenities:
- ☐ easy access ☐ back-in ☐ pull-through
- ☐ water ☐ pet friendly ☐ laundry
- ☐ paved ☐ sewer ☐ electricity
- ☐ 15 amp ☐ 30 amp ☐ 50 amp
- ☐ shade ☐ pool ☐ restrooms
- ☐ store ☐ picnic table ☐ fire ring
- ☐ firewood ☐ tv ☐ wifi
- ☐ security ☐ ice ☐ cafe

Activities:
- ☐ fishing ☐ hiking ☐ canoeing
- ☐ lake ☐ river ☐ hot tub
- ☐ fitness ☐ bike ☐ boat
- ☐ shuffleboard ☐ pickleball ☐ golf

Camped with:_____
_____
_____

People met:_____
_____

New friends:_____
_____

Places visited:_____
_____
_____

Visit/do next time:_____
_____
_____

Most memorable event:_____
_____
_____

Most fun things:_____
_____
_____
_____
_____

Notes:_____
_____
_____
_____
_____
_____
_____

Drawing or favorite photo:

Campground: _____ Dates: _____

Location: _____
Travel to Campground: *Miles:* _____ *Time:* _____ *Cost:* _____
Weather/Temperature: _____

Campground Information

Name: _____
Address: _____
Phone: _____
Site#: _____ Site for next time: _____
Cost: _____ $ ☐ Day ☐ Week ☐ Month
GPS: _____
Rating: ★☆☆☆☆☆☆☆☆☆
Water pressure ★☆☆☆☆ Location ★☆☆☆☆
Cleanliness   ★☆☆☆☆ Site size ★☆☆☆☆
Restrooms   ★☆☆☆☆ Noise   ★☆☆☆☆

Amenities:
☐ easy access   ☐ back-in   ☐ pull-through
☐ water   ☐ pet friendly ☐ laundry
☐ paved   ☐ sewer   ☐ electricity
☐ 15 amp   ☐ 30 amp   ☐ 50 amp
☐ shade   ☐ pool   ☐ restrooms
☐ store   ☐ picnic table ☐ fire ring
☐ firewood   ☐ tv   ☐ wifi
☐ security   ☐ ice   ☐ cafe

Activities:
☐ fishing   ☐ hiking   ☐ canoeing
☐ lake   ☐ river   ☐ hot tub
☐ fitness   ☐ bike   ☐ boat
☐ shuffleboard ☐ pickleball   ☐ golf

Camped with: _____
_____
_____

People met: _____
_____

New friends: _____
_____

Places visited: _____
_____
_____

Visit/do next time: _____
_____
_____

Most memorable event:_____
_____
_____

Most fun things:_____
_____
_____
_____
_____

Notes:_____
_____
_____
_____
_____
_____

Drawing or favorite photo:

Campground: _____ **Dates:** _____

Location: _____
Travel to Campground: *Miles:* _____ *Time:* _____ *Cost:* _____
Weather/Temperature: _____

Campground Information

Name: _____
Address: _____
Phone: _____
Site#: _____ Site for next time: _____
Cost: _____ $ ☐ Day ☐ Week ☐ Month
GPS: _____
Rating: ★☆☆☆☆☆☆☆☆☆
Water pressure ★☆☆☆☆ Location ★☆☆☆☆
Cleanliness   ★☆☆☆☆ Site size ★☆☆☆☆
Restrooms   ★☆☆☆☆ Noise   ★☆☆☆☆

Amenities:
- ☐ easy access ☐ back-in   ☐ pull-through
- ☐ water   ☐ pet friendly ☐ laundry
- ☐ paved   ☐ sewer   ☐ electricity
- ☐ 15 amp   ☐ 30 amp   ☐ 50 amp
- ☐ shade   ☐ pool   ☐ restrooms
- ☐ store   ☐ picnic table ☐ fire ring
- ☐ firewood   ☐ tv   ☐ wifi
- ☐ security   ☐ ice   ☐ cafe

Activities:
- ☐ fishing   ☐ hiking   ☐ canoeing
- ☐ lake   ☐ river   ☐ hot tub
- ☐ fitness   ☐ bike   ☐ boat
- ☐ shuffleboard ☐ pickleball ☐ golf

Camped with: _____
_____

People met: _____
_____

New friends: _____
_____

Places visited: _____
_____

Visit/do next time: _____
_____

Most memorable event:_____
_____
_____

Most fun things:_____
_____
_____
_____

Notes:_____
_____
_____
_____
_____
_____

Drawing or favorite photo:

Campground: _____ **Dates:** _____

Location: _____

Travel to Campground: *Miles:* _____ *Time:* _____ *Cost:* _____

Weather/Temperature: _____

Campground Information

Name: _____

Address: _____

Phone: _____

Site#: _____ Site for next time: _____

Cost: _____ $ ☐ Day ☐ Week ☐ Month

GPS: _____

Rating: ★☆☆☆☆☆☆☆☆☆

Water pressure ★☆☆☆☆   Location ★☆☆☆☆

Cleanliness ★☆☆☆☆   Site size ★☆☆☆☆

Restrooms ★☆☆☆☆   Noise ★☆☆☆☆

Amenities:
- ☐ easy access
- ☐ water
- ☐ paved
- ☐ 15 amp
- ☐ shade
- ☐ store
- ☐ firewood
- ☐ security
- ☐ back-in
- ☐ pet friendly
- ☐ sewer
- ☐ 30 amp
- ☐ pool
- ☐ picnic table
- ☐ tv
- ☐ ice
- ☐ pull-through
- ☐ laundry
- ☐ electricity
- ☐ 50 amp
- ☐ restrooms
- ☐ fire ring
- ☐ wifi
- ☐ cafe

Activities:
- ☐ fishing
- ☐ lake
- ☐ fitness
- ☐ shuffleboard
- ☐ hiking
- ☐ river
- ☐ bike
- ☐ pickleball
- ☐ canoeing
- ☐ hot tub
- ☐ boat
- ☐ golf

Camped with: _____
_____
_____

People met: _____
_____

New friends: _____
_____

Places visited: _____
_____
_____

Visit/do next time: _____
_____
_____

Most memorable event: _____
_____
_____

Most fun things: _____
_____
_____
_____

Notes: _____
_____
_____
_____
_____
_____

Drawing or favorite photo:

Campground: _____   Dates: _____

Location: _____
Travel to Campground: *Miles:* _____ *Time:* _____ *Cost:* _____
Weather/Temperature: _____

Campground Information

Name: _____
Address: _____
Phone: _____
Site#: _____ Site for next time: _____
Cost: _____ $ ☐ Day ☐ Week ☐ Month
GPS: _____
Rating: ★☆☆☆☆☆☆☆☆☆
Water pressure ★☆☆☆☆   Location ★☆☆☆☆
Cleanliness   ★☆☆☆☆   Site size ★☆☆☆☆
Restrooms   ★☆☆☆☆   Noise   ★☆☆☆☆

Amenities:
☐ easy access   ☐ back-in   ☐ pull-through
☐ water   ☐ pet friendly ☐ laundry
☐ paved   ☐ sewer   ☐ electricity
☐ 15 amp   ☐ 30 amp   ☐ 50 amp
☐ shade   ☐ pool   ☐ restrooms
☐ store   ☐ picnic table ☐ fire ring
☐ firewood   ☐ tv   ☐ wifi
☐ security   ☐ ice   ☐ cafe

Activities:
☐ fishing   ☐ hiking   ☐ canoeing
☐ lake   ☐ river   ☐ hot tub
☐ fitness   ☐ bike   ☐ boat
☐ shuffleboard ☐ pickleball   ☐ golf

Camped with: _____
_____
_____

People met: _____
_____

New friends: _____
_____

Places visited: _____
_____
_____

Visit/do next time: _____
_____
_____

Most memorable event: _____
_____
_____

Most fun things: _____
_____
_____
_____

Notes: _____
_____
_____
_____
_____
_____

Drawing or favorite photo:

Campground: _____ Dates: _____

Location: _____
Travel to Campground: *Miles:* _____ *Time:* _____ *Cost:* _____
Weather/Temperature: _____

Campground Information

Name: _____
Address: _____
Phone: _____
Site#: _____ Site for next time: _____
Cost: _____ $ ☐ Day ☐ Week ☐ Month
GPS: _____
Rating: ★☆☆☆☆☆☆☆
Water pressure ★☆☆☆☆ Location ★☆☆☆☆
Cleanliness ★☆☆☆☆ Site size ★☆☆☆☆
Restrooms ★☆☆☆☆ Noise ★☆☆☆☆

Amenities:
☐ easy access ☐ back-in ☐ pull-through
☐ water ☐ pet friendly ☐ laundry
☐ paved ☐ sewer ☐ electricity
☐ 15 amp ☐ 30 amp ☐ 50 amp
☐ shade ☐ pool ☐ restrooms
☐ store ☐ picnic table ☐ fire ring
☐ firewood ☐ tv ☐ wifi
☐ security ☐ ice ☐ cafe

Activities:
☐ fishing ☐ hiking ☐ canoeing
☐ lake ☐ river ☐ hot tub
☐ fitness ☐ bike ☐ boat
☐ shuffleboard ☐ pickleball ☐ golf

Camped with: _____
_____
_____

People met: _____
_____

New friends: _____
_____

Places visited: _____
_____
_____

Visit/do next time: _____
_____
_____

Most memorable event:_____
_____
_____

Most fun things:_____
_____
_____
_____

Notes:_____
_____
_____
_____
_____
_____

Drawing or favorite photo:

Campground: _____   **Dates:** _____

Location: _____
Travel to Campground: *Miles:* _____   *Time:* _____   *Cost:* _____
Weather/Temperature: _____

Campground Information

Name: _____
Address: _____
Phone: _____
Site#: _____   Site for next time: _____
Cost: _____ $ ☐ Day ☐ Week ☐ Month
GPS: _____
Rating: ★☆☆☆☆☆☆☆☆☆
Water pressure ★☆☆☆☆   Location ★☆☆☆☆
Cleanliness ★☆☆☆☆   Site size ★☆☆☆☆
Restrooms ★☆☆☆☆   Noise ★☆☆☆☆

Amenities:
- ☐ easy access   ☐ back-in   ☐ pull-through
- ☐ water   ☐ pet friendly   ☐ laundry
- ☐ paved   ☐ sewer   ☐ electricity
- ☐ 15 amp   ☐ 30 amp   ☐ 50 amp
- ☐ shade   ☐ pool   ☐ restrooms
- ☐ store   ☐ picnic table   ☐ fire ring
- ☐ firewood   ☐ tv   ☐ wifi
- ☐ security   ☐ ice   ☐ cafe

Activities:
- ☐ fishing   ☐ hiking   ☐ canoeing
- ☐ lake   ☐ river   ☐ hot tub
- ☐ fitness   ☐ bike   ☐ boat
- ☐ shuffleboard ☐ pickleball   ☐ golf

Camped with: _____
_____
_____

People met: _____
_____

New friends: _____
_____

Places visited: _____
_____
_____

Visit/do next time: _____
_____
_____

Most memorable event:_____
_____
_____

Most fun things:_____
_____
_____
_____

Notes:_____
_____
_____
_____
_____
_____

Drawing or favorite photo:

Campground: _____ **Dates:** _____

Location: _____

Travel to Campground: *Miles:*_____ *Time:*_____ *Cost:*_____

Weather/Temperature: _____

Campground Information

Name: _____

Address: _____

Phone: _____

Site#: _____ Site for next time: _____

Cost: _____ $ ☐ Day ☐ Week ☐ Month

GPS: _____

Rating: ★☆☆☆☆☆☆☆☆☆

Water pressure ★☆☆☆☆ Location ★☆☆☆☆

Cleanliness ★☆☆☆☆ Site size ★☆☆☆☆

Restrooms ★☆☆☆☆ Noise ★☆☆☆☆

Amenities:
- ☐ easy access   ☐ back-in   ☐ pull-through
- ☐ water   ☐ pet friendly   ☐ laundry
- ☐ paved   ☐ sewer   ☐ electricity
- ☐ 15 amp   ☐ 30 amp   ☐ 50 amp
- ☐ shade   ☐ pool   ☐ restrooms
- ☐ store   ☐ picnic table   ☐ fire ring
- ☐ firewood   ☐ tv   ☐ wifi
- ☐ security   ☐ ice   ☐ cafe

Activities:
- ☐ fishing   ☐ hiking   ☐ canoeing
- ☐ lake   ☐ river   ☐ hot tub
- ☐ fitness   ☐ bike   ☐ boat
- ☐ shuffleboard ☐ pickleball   ☐ golf

Camped with: _____
_____
_____

People met: _____
_____

New friends: _____
_____

Places visited: _____
_____
_____

Visit/do next time: _____
_____
_____

Most memorable event:_____
_____
_____

Most fun things:_____
_____
_____
_____

Notes:_____
_____
_____
_____
_____
_____

Drawing or favorite photo:

Campground: _____   **Dates:** _____

Location: _____
Travel to Campground: *Miles:* _____ *Time:* _____ *Cost:* _____
Weather/Temperature: _____

Campground Information

Name: _____
Address: _____
Phone: _____
Site#: _____ Site for next time: _____
Cost: _____ $ ☐ Day ☐ Week ☐ Month
GPS: _____
Rating: ★☆☆☆☆☆☆☆☆☆
Water pressure ★☆☆☆☆ Location ★☆☆☆☆
Cleanliness   ★☆☆☆☆ Site size ★☆☆☆☆
Restrooms   ★☆☆☆☆ Noise   ★☆☆☆☆

Amenities:
☐ easy access   ☐ back-in   ☐ pull-through
☐ water   ☐ pet friendly   ☐ laundry
☐ paved   ☐ sewer   ☐ electricity
☐ 15 amp   ☐ 30 amp   ☐ 50 amp
☐ shade   ☐ pool   ☐ restrooms
☐ store   ☐ picnic table   ☐ fire ring
☐ firewood   ☐ tv   ☐ wifi
☐ security   ☐ ice   ☐ cafe

Activities:
☐ fishing   ☐ hiking   ☐ canoeing
☐ lake   ☐ river   ☐ hot tub
☐ fitness   ☐ bike   ☐ boat
☐ shuffleboard ☐ pickleball   ☐ golf

Camped with: _____
_____
_____

People met: _____
_____

New friends: _____
_____

Places visited: _____
_____
_____

Visit/do next time: _____
_____
_____

Most memorable event:_____
_____
_____

Most fun things:_____
_____
_____
_____

Notes:_____
_____
_____
_____
_____
_____

Drawing or favorite photo:

Campground: _____   Dates: _____

Location: _____
Travel to Campground: *Miles:* _____ *Time:* _____ *Cost:* _____
Weather/Temperature: _____

Campground Information

Name: _____

Address: _____

Phone: _____

Site#: _____ Site for next time: _____

Cost: _____ $ ☐ Day ☐ Week ☐ Month

GPS: _____

Rating: ★☆☆☆☆☆☆☆☆☆

Water pressure ★☆☆☆☆   Location ★☆☆☆☆

Cleanliness   ★☆☆☆☆   Site size ★☆☆☆☆

Restrooms   ★☆☆☆☆   Noise   ★☆☆☆☆

Amenities:
- ☐ easy access ☐ back-in   ☐ pull-through
- ☐ water   ☐ pet friendly ☐ laundry
- ☐ paved   ☐ sewer   ☐ electricity
- ☐ 15 amp   ☐ 30 amp   ☐ 50 amp
- ☐ shade   ☐ pool   ☐ restrooms
- ☐ store   ☐ picnic table ☐ fire ring
- ☐ firewood   ☐ tv   ☐ wifi
- ☐ security   ☐ ice   ☐ cafe

Activities:
- ☐ fishing   ☐ hiking   ☐ canoeing
- ☐ lake   ☐ river   ☐ hot tub
- ☐ fitness   ☐ bike   ☐ boat
- ☐ shuffleboard ☐ pickleball   ☐ golf

Camped with: _____
_____
_____

People met: _____
_____

New friends: _____
_____

Places visited: _____
_____
_____

Visit/do next time: _____
_____
_____

Most memorable event:

Most fun things:

Notes:

Drawing or favorite photo:

Campground: _____   Dates: _____

Location: _____
Travel to Campground: *Miles:* _____ *Time:* _____ *Cost:* _____
Weather/Temperature: _____

Campground Information

Name: _____
Address: _____
Phone: _____
Site#: _____ Site for next time: _____
Cost: _____ $ ☐ Day ☐ Week ☐ Month
GPS: _____
Rating: ★☆☆☆☆☆☆☆☆☆
Water pressure ★☆☆☆☆ Location ★☆☆☆☆
Cleanliness   ★☆☆☆☆ Site size ★☆☆☆☆
Restrooms   ★☆☆☆☆ Noise   ★☆☆☆☆

Amenities:
☐ easy access   ☐ back-in   ☐ pull-through
☐ water   ☐ pet friendly   ☐ laundry
☐ paved   ☐ sewer   ☐ electricity
☐ 15 amp   ☐ 30 amp   ☐ 50 amp
☐ shade   ☐ pool   ☐ restrooms
☐ store   ☐ picnic table   ☐ fire ring
☐ firewood   ☐ tv   ☐ wifi
☐ security   ☐ ice   ☐ cafe

Activities:
☐ fishing   ☐ hiking   ☐ canoeing
☐ lake   ☐ river   ☐ hot tub
☐ fitness   ☐ bike   ☐ boat
☐ shuffleboard   ☐ pickleball   ☐ golf

Camped with: _____
_____
_____

People met: _____
_____

New friends: _____
_____

Places visited: _____
_____
_____

Visit/do next time: _____
_____
_____

Most memorable event:_____
_____
_____

Most fun things:_____
_____
_____
_____

Notes:_____
_____
_____
_____
_____
_____

Drawing or favorite photo:

Campground: _____ **Dates:** _____

Location: _____
Travel to Campground: *Miles:* _____ *Time:* _____ *Cost:* _____
Weather/Temperature: _____

Campground Information

Name: _____
Address: _____
Phone: _____
Site#: _____ Site for next time: _____
Cost: _____ $ ☐ Day ☐ Week ☐ Month
GPS: _____
Rating: ★☆☆☆☆☆☆☆☆☆
Water pressure ★☆☆☆☆ Location ★☆☆☆☆
Cleanliness   ★☆☆☆☆ Site size ★☆☆☆☆
Restrooms   ★☆☆☆☆ Noise   ★☆☆☆☆

Amenities:
☐ easy access   ☐ back-in   ☐ pull-through
☐ water   ☐ pet friendly   ☐ laundry
☐ paved   ☐ sewer   ☐ electricity
☐ 15 amp   ☐ 30 amp   ☐ 50 amp
☐ shade   ☐ pool   ☐ restrooms
☐ store   ☐ picnic table   ☐ fire ring
☐ firewood   ☐ tv   ☐ wifi
☐ security   ☐ ice   ☐ cafe

Activities:
☐ fishing   ☐ hiking   ☐ canoeing
☐ lake   ☐ river   ☐ hot tub
☐ fitness   ☐ bike   ☐ boat
☐ shuffleboard   ☐ pickleball   ☐ golf

Camped with: _____
_____
_____

People met: _____
_____

New friends: _____
_____

Places visited: _____
_____
_____

Visit/do next time: _____
_____
_____

Most memorable event:

Most fun things:

Notes:

Drawing or favorite photo:

Campground: _____ Dates: _____

Location:_____
Travel to Campground: *Miles:*_____ *Time:*_____ *Cost:*_____
Weather/Temperature:_____

Campground Information

Name:_____
Address:_____
Phone:_____
Site#:_____ Site for next time:_____
Cost:_____ $ ☐ Day ☐ Week ☐ Month
GPS:_____
Rating: ★☆☆☆☆☆☆☆☆☆
Water pressure ★☆☆☆☆ Location ★☆☆☆☆
Cleanliness ★☆☆☆☆ Site size ★☆☆☆☆
Restrooms ★☆☆☆☆ Noise ★☆☆☆☆

Amenities:
- ☐ easy access
- ☐ back-in
- ☐ pull-through
- ☐ water
- ☐ pet friendly
- ☐ laundry
- ☐ paved
- ☐ sewer
- ☐ electricity
- ☐ 15 amp
- ☐ 30 amp
- ☐ 50 amp
- ☐ shade
- ☐ pool
- ☐ restrooms
- ☐ store
- ☐ picnic table
- ☐ fire ring
- ☐ firewood
- ☐ tv
- ☐ wifi
- ☐ security
- ☐ ice
- ☐ cafe

Activities:
- ☐ fishing
- ☐ hiking
- ☐ canoeing
- ☐ lake
- ☐ river
- ☐ hot tub
- ☐ fitness
- ☐ bike
- ☐ boat
- ☐ shuffleboard
- ☐ pickleball
- ☐ golf

Camped with:_____
_____
_____

People met:_____
_____

New friends:_____
_____

Places visited:_____
_____
_____

Visit/do next time:_____
_____
_____

Most memorable event: _____
_____
_____

Most fun things: _____
_____
_____
_____

Notes: _____
_____
_____
_____
_____
_____

Drawing or favorite photo:

Campground: _____   **Dates:** _____

Location: _____
Travel to Campground: *Miles:* _____ *Time:* _____ *Cost:* _____
Weather/Temperature: _____

Campground Information

Name: _____
Address: _____
Phone: _____
Site#: _____ Site for next time: _____
Cost: _____ $ ☐ Day ☐ Week ☐ Month
GPS: _____
Rating: ★☆☆☆☆☆☆☆☆☆
Water pressure ★☆☆☆☆   Location   ★☆☆☆☆
Cleanliness   ★☆☆☆☆   Site size ★☆☆☆☆
Restrooms   ★☆☆☆☆   Noise   ★☆☆☆☆

Amenities:
☐ easy access   ☐ back-in   ☐ pull-through
☐ water   ☐ pet friendly   ☐ laundry
☐ paved   ☐ sewer   ☐ electricity
☐ 15 amp   ☐ 30 amp   ☐ 50 amp
☐ shade   ☐ pool   ☐ restrooms
☐ store   ☐ picnic table   ☐ fire ring
☐ firewood   ☐ tv   ☐ wifi
☐ security   ☐ ice   ☐ cafe

Activities:
☐ fishing   ☐ hiking   ☐ canoeing
☐ lake   ☐ river   ☐ hot tub
☐ fitness   ☐ bike   ☐ boat
☐ shuffleboard   ☐ pickleball   ☐ golf

Camped with: _____
_____
_____

People met: _____
_____

New friends: _____
_____

Places visited: _____
_____
_____

Visit/do next time: _____
_____
_____

Most memorable event:_____
_____
_____

Most fun things:_____
_____
_____
_____
_____

Notes:_____
_____
_____
_____
_____
_____

Drawing or favorite photo:

Campground: _____   Dates: _____

Location: _____
Travel to Campground: *Miles:* _____   *Time:* _____   *Cost:* _____
Weather/Temperature: _____

Campground Information

Name: _____
Address: _____
Phone: _____
Site#: _____ Site for next time: _____
Cost: _____ $ ☐ Day ☐ Week ☐ Month
GPS: _____
Rating: ★☆☆☆☆☆☆☆☆☆
Water pressure ★☆☆☆☆   Location ★☆☆☆☆
Cleanliness   ★☆☆☆☆   Site size ★☆☆☆☆
Restrooms   ★☆☆☆☆   Noise   ★☆☆☆☆

Amenities:
☐ easy access   ☐ back-in   ☐ pull-through
☐ water   ☐ pet friendly   ☐ laundry
☐ paved   ☐ sewer   ☐ electricity
☐ 15 amp   ☐ 30 amp   ☐ 50 amp
☐ shade   ☐ pool   ☐ restrooms
☐ store   ☐ picnic table   ☐ fire ring
☐ firewood   ☐ tv   ☐ wifi
☐ security   ☐ ice   ☐ cafe

Activities:
☐ fishing   ☐ hiking   ☐ canoeing
☐ lake   ☐ river   ☐ hot tub
☐ fitness   ☐ bike   ☐ boat
☐ shuffleboard ☐ pickleball   ☐ golf

Camped with: _____
_____
_____

People met: _____
_____

New friends: _____
_____

Places visited: _____
_____
_____

Visit/do next time: _____
_____
_____

Most memorable event:_____
_____
_____

Most fun things:_____
_____
_____
_____

Notes:_____
_____
_____
_____
_____
_____
_____

Drawing or favorite photo:

Campground: _____ **Dates:** _____

Location: _____

Travel to Campground: *Miles:* _____   *Time:* _____   *Cost:* _____

Weather/Temperature: _____

Campground Information

Name: _____

Address: _____

Phone: _____

Site#: _____ Site for next time: _____

Cost: _____ $ ☐ Day ☐ Week ☐ Month

GPS: _____

Rating: ★☆☆☆☆☆☆☆☆☆

Water pressure ★☆☆☆☆   Location ★☆☆☆☆

Cleanliness ★☆☆☆☆   Site size ★☆☆☆☆

Restrooms ★☆☆☆☆   Noise ★☆☆☆☆

Amenities:
- ☐ easy access   ☐ back-in   ☐ pull-through
- ☐ water   ☐ pet friendly   ☐ laundry
- ☐ paved   ☐ sewer   ☐ electricity
- ☐ 15 amp   ☐ 30 amp   ☐ 50 amp
- ☐ shade   ☐ pool   ☐ restrooms
- ☐ store   ☐ picnic table   ☐ fire ring
- ☐ firewood   ☐ tv   ☐ wifi
- ☐ security   ☐ ice   ☐ cafe

Activities:
- ☐ fishing   ☐ hiking   ☐ canoeing
- ☐ lake   ☐ river   ☐ hot tub
- ☐ fitness   ☐ bike   ☐ boat
- ☐ shuffleboard   ☐ pickleball   ☐ golf

Camped with: _____
_____
_____

People met: _____
_____

New friends: _____
_____

Places visited: _____
_____
_____

Visit/do next time: _____
_____
_____

Most memorable event:_____
_____
_____

Most fun things:_____
_____
_____
_____

Notes:_____
_____
_____
_____
_____
_____

Drawing or favorite photo:

Campground:	Dates:

Location: _____
Travel to Campground: *Miles:* _____ *Time:* _____ *Cost:* _____
Weather/Temperature: _____

Campground Information

Name: _____
Address: _____
Phone: _____
Site#: _____ Site for next time: _____
Cost: _____ $ ☐ Day ☐ Week ☐ Month
GPS: _____
Rating: ★☆☆☆☆☆☆☆☆☆
Water pressure ★☆☆☆☆ Location ★☆☆☆☆
Cleanliness ★☆☆☆☆ Site size ★☆☆☆☆
Restrooms ★☆☆☆☆ Noise ★☆☆☆☆

Amenities:
☐ easy access ☐ back-in ☐ pull-through
☐ water ☐ pet friendly ☐ laundry
☐ paved ☐ sewer ☐ electricity
☐ 15 amp ☐ 30 amp ☐ 50 amp
☐ shade ☐ pool ☐ restrooms
☐ store ☐ picnic table ☐ fire ring
☐ firewood ☐ tv ☐ wifi
☐ security ☐ ice ☐ cafe

Activities:
☐ fishing ☐ hiking ☐ canoeing
☐ lake ☐ river ☐ hot tub
☐ fitness ☐ bike ☐ boat
☐ shuffleboard ☐ pickleball ☐ golf

Camped with: _____
_____
_____

People met: _____
_____

New friends: _____
_____

Places visited: _____
_____
_____

Visit/do next time: _____
_____
_____

Most memorable event:_____
_____
_____

Most fun things:_____
_____
_____
_____

Notes:_____
_____
_____
_____
_____
_____

Drawing or favorite photo:

Campground: _____   Dates: _____

Location: _____
Travel to Campground: *Miles:* _____ *Time:* _____ *Cost:* _____
Weather/Temperature: _____

Campground Information

Name: _____
Address: _____
Phone: _____
Site#: _____ Site for next time: _____
Cost: _____ $ ☐ Day ☐ Week ☐ Month
GPS: _____
Rating: ★☆☆☆☆☆☆☆☆☆
Water pressure ★☆☆☆☆   Location ★☆☆☆☆
Cleanliness   ★☆☆☆☆   Site size ★☆☆☆☆
Restrooms   ★☆☆☆☆   Noise   ★☆☆☆☆

Amenities:
☐ easy access   ☐ back-in   ☐ pull-through
☐ water   ☐ pet friendly   ☐ laundry
☐ paved   ☐ sewer   ☐ electricity
☐ 15 amp   ☐ 30 amp   ☐ 50 amp
☐ shade   ☐ pool   ☐ restrooms
☐ store   ☐ picnic table   ☐ fire ring
☐ firewood   ☐ tv   ☐ wifi
☐ security   ☐ ice   ☐ cafe

Activities:
☐ fishing   ☐ hiking   ☐ canoeing
☐ lake   ☐ river   ☐ hot tub
☐ fitness   ☐ bike   ☐ boat
☐ shuffleboard ☐ pickleball   ☐ golf

Camped with: _____
_____
_____

People met: _____
_____
_____

New friends: _____
_____
_____

Places visited: _____
_____
_____

Visit/do next time: _____
_____
_____

Most memorable event: _____
_____
_____

Most fun things: _____
_____
_____
_____

Notes: _____
_____
_____
_____
_____
_____

Drawing or favorite photo:

Campground: _____ Dates: _____

Location: _____
Travel to Campground: *Miles:* _____ *Time:* _____ *Cost:* _____
Weather/Temperature: _____

Campground Information

Name: _____
Address: _____
Phone: _____
Site#: _____ Site for next time: _____
Cost: _____ $ ☐ Day ☐ Week ☐ Month
GPS: _____
Rating: ★☆☆☆☆☆☆☆☆☆
Water pressure ★☆☆☆☆ Location ★☆☆☆☆
Cleanliness ★☆☆☆☆ Site size ★☆☆☆☆
Restrooms ★☆☆☆☆ Noise ★☆☆☆☆

Amenities:
☐ easy access ☐ back-in ☐ pull-through
☐ water ☐ pet friendly ☐ laundry
☐ paved ☐ sewer ☐ electricity
☐ 15 amp ☐ 30 amp ☐ 50 amp
☐ shade ☐ pool ☐ restrooms
☐ store ☐ picnic table ☐ fire ring
☐ firewood ☐ tv ☐ wifi
☐ security ☐ ice ☐ cafe

Activities:
☐ fishing ☐ hiking ☐ canoeing
☐ lake ☐ river ☐ hot tub
☐ fitness ☐ bike ☐ boat
☐ shuffleboard ☐ pickleball ☐ golf

Camped with: _____
_____
_____

People met: _____
_____

New friends: _____
_____

Places visited: _____
_____
_____

Visit/do next time: _____
_____
_____

Most memorable event:_____
_____
_____

Most fun things:_____
_____
_____
_____

Notes:_____
_____
_____
_____
_____
_____

Drawing or favorite photo:

Campground:	Dates:

Location:_____
Travel to Campground: *Miles:*_____ *Time:*_____ *Cost:*_____
Weather/Temperature:_____

Campground Information

Name:_____
Address:_____
Phone:_____
Site#:_____ Site for next time:_____
Cost:_____ $ ☐ Day ☐ Week ☐ Month
GPS:_____
Rating: ★☆☆☆☆☆☆☆☆☆
Water pressure ★☆☆☆☆ Location ★☆☆☆☆
Cleanliness ★☆☆☆☆ Site size ★☆☆☆☆
Restrooms ★☆☆☆☆ Noise ★☆☆☆☆

Amenities:
- ☐ easy access   ☐ back-in   ☐ pull-through
- ☐ water   ☐ pet friendly   ☐ laundry
- ☐ paved   ☐ sewer   ☐ electricity
- ☐ 15 amp   ☐ 30 amp   ☐ 50 amp
- ☐ shade   ☐ pool   ☐ restrooms
- ☐ store   ☐ picnic table   ☐ fire ring
- ☐ firewood   ☐ tv   ☐ wifi
- ☐ security   ☐ ice   ☐ cafe

Activities:
- ☐ fishing   ☐ hiking   ☐ canoeing
- ☐ lake   ☐ river   ☐ hot tub
- ☐ fitness   ☐ bike   ☐ boat
- ☐ shuffleboard ☐ pickleball   ☐ golf

Camped with:_____
_____
_____

People met:_____
_____

New friends:_____
_____

Places visited:_____
_____
_____

Visit/do next time:_____
_____
_____

Most memorable event:_____
_____
_____

Most fun things:_____
_____
_____
_____

Notes:_____
_____
_____
_____
_____
_____

Drawing or favorite photo:

Campground: _____ **Dates:** _____

Location:_____

Travel to Campground: *Miles:*_____ *Time:*_____ *Cost:*_____

Weather/Temperature:_____

Campground Information

Name:_____

Address:_____

Phone:_____

Site#:_____ Site for next time:_____

Cost:_____ $ ☐ Day ☐ Week ☐ Month

GPS:_____

Rating: ★☆☆☆☆☆☆☆☆☆

Water pressure ★☆☆☆☆ Location ★☆☆☆☆

Cleanliness ★☆☆☆☆ Site size ★☆☆☆☆

Restrooms ★☆☆☆☆ Noise ★☆☆☆☆

Amenities:
- ☐ easy access
- ☐ water
- ☐ paved
- ☐ 15 amp
- ☐ shade
- ☐ store
- ☐ firewood
- ☐ security
- ☐ back-in
- ☐ pet friendly
- ☐ sewer
- ☐ 30 amp
- ☐ pool
- ☐ picnic table
- ☐ tv
- ☐ ice
- ☐ pull-through
- ☐ laundry
- ☐ electricity
- ☐ 50 amp
- ☐ restrooms
- ☐ fire ring
- ☐ wifi
- ☐ cafe

Activities:
- ☐ fishing
- ☐ lake
- ☐ fitness
- ☐ shuffleboard
- ☐ hiking
- ☐ river
- ☐ bike
- ☐ pickleball
- ☐ canoeing
- ☐ hot tub
- ☐ boat
- ☐ golf

Camped with:_____
_____
_____

People met:_____
_____

New friends:_____
_____

Places visited:_____
_____
_____

Visit/do next time:_____
_____
_____

Most memorable event: _____
_____
_____

Most fun things: _____
_____
_____
_____

Notes: _____
_____
_____
_____
_____
_____

Drawing or favorite photo:

Campground: _____ **Dates:** _____

Location:_____
Travel to Campground: *Miles:*_____ *Time:*_____ *Cost:*_____
Weather/Temperature:_____

Campground Information

Name:_____
Address:_____
Phone:_____
Site#:_____ Site for next time:_____
Cost:_____ $ ☐ Day ☐ Week ☐ Month
GPS:_____
Rating: ★☆☆☆☆☆☆☆☆☆
Water pressure ★☆☆☆☆ Location ★☆☆☆☆
Cleanliness   ★☆☆☆☆ Site size ★☆☆☆☆
Restrooms   ★☆☆☆☆ Noise   ★☆☆☆☆

Amenities:
☐ easy access   ☐ back-in   ☐ pull-through
☐ water   ☐ pet friendly   ☐ laundry
☐ paved   ☐ sewer   ☐ electricity
☐ 15 amp   ☐ 30 amp   ☐ 50 amp
☐ shade   ☐ pool   ☐ restrooms
☐ store   ☐ picnic table   ☐ fire ring
☐ firewood   ☐ tv   ☐ wifi
☐ security   ☐ ice   ☐ cafe

Activities:
☐ fishing   ☐ hiking   ☐ canoeing
☐ lake   ☐ river   ☐ hot tub
☐ fitness   ☐ bike   ☐ boat
☐ shuffleboard ☐ pickleball   ☐ golf

Camped with:_____
_____
_____

People met:_____
_____

New friends:_____
_____

Places visited:_____
_____
_____

Visit/do next time:_____
_____
_____

Most memorable event:_____
_____
_____

Most fun things:_____
_____
_____
_____

Notes:_____
_____
_____
_____
_____
_____

Drawing or favorite photo:

Campground: _____ **Dates:** _____

Location: _____
Travel to Campground: *Miles:* _____ *Time:* _____ *Cost:* _____
Weather/Temperature: _____

Campground Information

Name: _____
Address: _____
Phone: _____
Site#: _____ Site for next time: _____
Cost: _____ $ ☐ Day ☐ Week ☐ Month
GPS: _____
Rating: ★☆☆☆☆☆☆☆☆☆
Water pressure ★☆☆☆☆ Location ★☆☆☆☆
Cleanliness   ★☆☆☆☆ Site size ★☆☆☆☆
Restrooms   ★☆☆☆☆ Noise   ★☆☆☆☆

Amenities:
☐ easy access   ☐ back-in   ☐ pull-through
☐ water   ☐ pet friendly   ☐ laundry
☐ paved   ☐ sewer   ☐ electricity
☐ 15 amp   ☐ 30 amp   ☐ 50 amp
☐ shade   ☐ pool   ☐ restrooms
☐ store   ☐ picnic table   ☐ fire ring
☐ firewood   ☐ tv   ☐ wifi
☐ security   ☐ ice   ☐ cafe

Activities:
☐ fishing   ☐ hiking   ☐ canoeing
☐ lake   ☐ river   ☐ hot tub
☐ fitness   ☐ bike   ☐ boat
☐ shuffleboard   ☐ pickleball   ☐ golf

Camped with: _____
_____
_____

People met: _____
_____

New friends: _____
_____

Places visited: _____
_____
_____

Visit/do next time: _____
_____
_____

Most memorable event: _____
_____
_____

Most fun things: _____
_____
_____
_____

Notes: _____
_____
_____
_____
_____
_____

Drawing or favorite photo:

Campground: _____ **Dates:** _____

Location: _____

Travel to Campground: *Miles:* _____ *Time:* _____ *Cost:* _____

Weather/Temperature: _____

Campground Information

Name: _____

Address: _____

Phone: _____

Site#: _____ Site for next time: _____

Cost: _____ $ ☐ Day ☐ Week ☐ Month

GPS: _____

Rating: ★☆☆☆☆☆☆☆☆☆

Water pressure ★☆☆☆☆   Location ★☆☆☆☆

Cleanliness ★☆☆☆☆   Site size ★☆☆☆☆

Restrooms ★☆☆☆☆   Noise ★☆☆☆☆

Amenities:
- ☐ easy access ☐ back-in ☐ pull-through
- ☐ water ☐ pet friendly ☐ laundry
- ☐ paved ☐ sewer ☐ electricity
- ☐ 15 amp ☐ 30 amp ☐ 50 amp
- ☐ shade ☐ pool ☐ restrooms
- ☐ store ☐ picnic table ☐ fire ring
- ☐ firewood ☐ tv ☐ wifi
- ☐ security ☐ ice ☐ cafe

Activities:
- ☐ fishing ☐ hiking ☐ canoeing
- ☐ lake ☐ river ☐ hot tub
- ☐ fitness ☐ bike ☐ boat
- ☐ shuffleboard ☐ pickleball ☐ golf

Camped with: _____

_____

People met: _____

_____

New friends: _____

_____

Places visited: _____

_____

Visit/do next time: _____

_____

Most memorable event:_____
_____
_____

Most fun things:_____
_____
_____
_____

Notes:_____
_____
_____
_____
_____

Drawing or favorite photo:

Campground: _____ **Dates:** _____

Location: _____
Travel to Campground: *Miles:* _____ *Time:* _____ *Cost:* _____
Weather/Temperature: _____

Campground Information

Name: _____
Address: _____
Phone: _____
Site#: _____ Site for next time: _____
Cost: _____ $ ☐ Day ☐ Week ☐ Month
GPS: _____
Rating: ★☆☆☆☆☆☆☆☆☆
Water pressure ★☆☆☆☆ Location ★☆☆☆☆
Cleanliness ★☆☆☆☆ Site size ★☆☆☆☆
Restrooms ★☆☆☆☆ Noise ★☆☆☆☆

Amenities:
- ☐ easy access   ☐ back-in   ☐ pull-through
- ☐ water   ☐ pet friendly   ☐ laundry
- ☐ paved   ☐ sewer   ☐ electricity
- ☐ 15 amp   ☐ 30 amp   ☐ 50 amp
- ☐ shade   ☐ pool   ☐ restrooms
- ☐ store   ☐ picnic table   ☐ fire ring
- ☐ firewood   ☐ tv   ☐ wifi
- ☐ security   ☐ ice   ☐ cafe

Activities:
- ☐ fishing   ☐ hiking   ☐ canoeing
- ☐ lake   ☐ river   ☐ hot tub
- ☐ fitness   ☐ bike   ☐ boat
- ☐ shuffleboard ☐ pickleball   ☐ golf

Camped with: _____
_____
_____

People met: _____
_____

New friends: _____
_____

Places visited: _____
_____
_____

Visit/do next time: _____
_____
_____

Most memorable event:_____
_____
_____

Most fun things:_____
_____
_____
_____

Notes:_____
_____
_____
_____
_____
_____

Drawing or favorite photo:

Campground: _____ **Dates:** _____

Location:_____
Travel to Campground: *Miles:*_____ *Time:*_____ *Cost:*_____
Weather/Temperature:_____

Campground Information

Name:_____
Address:_____
Phone:_____
Site#:_____ Site for next time:_____
Cost:_____ $ ☐ Day ☐ Week ☐ Month
GPS:_____
Rating: ★☆☆☆☆☆☆☆☆☆
Water pressure ★☆☆☆☆ Location ★☆☆☆☆
Cleanliness ★☆☆☆☆ Site size ★☆☆☆☆
Restrooms ★☆☆☆☆ Noise ★☆☆☆☆

Amenities:
☐ easy access ☐ back-in ☐ pull-through
☐ water ☐ pet friendly ☐ laundry
☐ paved ☐ sewer ☐ electricity
☐ 15 amp ☐ 30 amp ☐ 50 amp
☐ shade ☐ pool ☐ restrooms
☐ store ☐ picnic table ☐ fire ring
☐ firewood ☐ tv ☐ wifi
☐ security ☐ ice ☐ cafe

Activities:
☐ fishing ☐ hiking ☐ canoeing
☐ lake ☐ river ☐ hot tub
☐ fitness ☐ bike ☐ boat
☐ shuffleboard ☐ pickleball ☐ golf

Camped with:_____
_____
_____

People met:_____
_____

New friends:_____
_____

Places visited:_____
_____
_____

Visit/do next time:_____
_____
_____

Most memorable event: _____
_____
_____

Most fun things: _____
_____
_____
_____

Notes: _____
_____
_____
_____
_____
_____

Drawing or favorite photo:

Campground: _____ **Dates:** _____

Location: _____
Travel to Campground: *Miles:* _____ *Time:* _____ *Cost:* _____
Weather/Temperature: _____

Campground Information

Name: _____
Address: _____
Phone: _____
Site#: _____ Site for next time: _____
Cost: _____ $ ☐ Day ☐ Week ☐ Month
GPS: _____
Rating: ★☆☆☆☆☆☆☆☆☆
Water pressure ★☆☆☆☆ Location ★☆☆☆☆
Cleanliness   ★☆☆☆☆ Site size ★☆☆☆☆
Restrooms   ★☆☆☆☆ Noise   ★☆☆☆☆

Amenities:
☐ easy access   ☐ back-in   ☐ pull-through
☐ water   ☐ pet friendly   ☐ laundry
☐ paved   ☐ sewer   ☐ electricity
☐ 15 amp   ☐ 30 amp   ☐ 50 amp
☐ shade   ☐ pool   ☐ restrooms
☐ store   ☐ picnic table   ☐ fire ring
☐ firewood   ☐ tv   ☐ wifi
☐ security   ☐ ice   ☐ cafe

Activities:
☐ fishing   ☐ hiking   ☐ canoeing
☐ lake   ☐ river   ☐ hot tub
☐ fitness   ☐ bike   ☐ boat
☐ shuffleboard ☐ pickleball   ☐ golf

Camped with: _____
_____
_____

People met: _____
_____

New friends: _____
_____

Places visited: _____
_____
_____

Visit/do next time: _____
_____
_____

Most memorable event:_____
_____
_____

Most fun things:_____
_____
_____
_____

Notes:_____
_____
_____
_____
_____

Drawing or favorite photo:

Campground: _____ **Dates:** _____

Location: _____
Travel to Campground: *Miles:* _____ *Time:* _____ *Cost:* _____
Weather/Temperature: _____

Campground Information

Name: _____
Address: _____
Phone: _____
Site#: _____ Site for next time: _____
Cost: _____ $ ☐ Day ☐ Week ☐ Month
GPS: _____
Rating: ★☆☆☆☆☆☆☆☆☆
Water pressure ★☆☆☆☆ Location ★☆☆☆☆
Cleanliness ★☆☆☆☆ Site size ★☆☆☆☆
Restrooms ★☆☆☆☆ Noise ★☆☆☆☆

Amenities:
☐ easy access ☐ back-in ☐ pull-through
☐ water ☐ pet friendly ☐ laundry
☐ paved ☐ sewer ☐ electricity
☐ 15 amp ☐ 30 amp ☐ 50 amp
☐ shade ☐ pool ☐ restrooms
☐ store ☐ picnic table ☐ fire ring
☐ firewood ☐ tv ☐ wifi
☐ security ☐ ice ☐ cafe

Activities:
☐ fishing ☐ hiking ☐ canoeing
☐ lake ☐ river ☐ hot tub
☐ fitness ☐ bike ☐ boat
☐ shuffleboard ☐ pickleball ☐ golf

Camped with: _____
_____
_____

People met: _____
_____
_____

New friends: _____
_____
_____

Places visited: _____
_____
_____

Visit/do next time: _____
_____
_____

Most memorable event:_____
_____
_____

Most fun things:_____
_____
_____
_____

Notes:_____
_____
_____
_____
_____
_____

Drawing or favorite photo:

Campground: _____ **Dates:** _____

Location: _____

Travel to Campground: *Miles:* _____ *Time:* _____ *Cost:* _____

Weather/Temperature: _____

Campground Information

Name: _____

Address: _____

Phone: _____

Site#: _____ Site for next time: _____

Cost: _____ $ ☐ Day ☐ Week ☐ Month

GPS: _____

Rating: ★☆☆☆☆☆☆☆☆☆

Water pressure ★☆☆☆☆ Location ★☆☆☆☆
Cleanliness ★☆☆☆☆ Site size ★☆☆☆☆
Restrooms ★☆☆☆☆ Noise ★☆☆☆☆

Amenities:
- ☐ easy access ☐ back-in ☐ pull-through
- ☐ water ☐ pet friendly ☐ laundry
- ☐ paved ☐ sewer ☐ electricity
- ☐ 15 amp ☐ 30 amp ☐ 50 amp
- ☐ shade ☐ pool ☐ restrooms
- ☐ store ☐ picnic table ☐ fire ring
- ☐ firewood ☐ tv ☐ wifi
- ☐ security ☐ ice ☐ cafe

Activities:
- ☐ fishing ☐ hiking ☐ canoeing
- ☐ lake ☐ river ☐ hot tub
- ☐ fitness ☐ bike ☐ boat
- ☐ shuffleboard ☐ pickleball ☐ golf

Camped with: _____
_____
_____

People met: _____
_____

New friends: _____
_____

Places visited: _____
_____
_____

Visit/do next time: _____
_____
_____

Most memorable event:_____
_____
_____

Most fun things:_____
_____
_____
_____

Notes:_____
_____
_____
_____
_____

Drawing or favorite photo:

Campground: _____ **Dates:** _____

Location: _____
Travel to Campground: *Miles:* _____ *Time:* _____ *Cost:* _____
Weather/Temperature: _____

Campground Information

Name: _____
Address: _____
Phone: _____
Site#: _____ Site for next time: _____
Cost: _____ $ ☐ Day ☐ Week ☐ Month
GPS: _____
Rating: ★☆☆☆☆☆☆☆☆☆
Water pressure ★☆☆☆☆ Location ★☆☆☆☆
Cleanliness ★☆☆☆☆ Site size ★☆☆☆☆
Restrooms ★☆☆☆☆ Noise ★☆☆☆☆

Amenities:
☐ easy access   ☐ back-in   ☐ pull-through
☐ water   ☐ pet friendly   ☐ laundry
☐ paved   ☐ sewer   ☐ electricity
☐ 15 amp   ☐ 30 amp   ☐ 50 amp
☐ shade   ☐ pool   ☐ restrooms
☐ store   ☐ picnic table   ☐ fire ring
☐ firewood   ☐ tv   ☐ wifi
☐ security   ☐ ice   ☐ cafe

Activities:
☐ fishing   ☐ hiking   ☐ canoeing
☐ lake   ☐ river   ☐ hot tub
☐ fitness   ☐ bike   ☐ boat
☐ shuffleboard   ☐ pickleball ☐ golf

Camped with: _____
_____
_____

People met: _____
_____

New friends: _____
_____

Places visited: _____
_____
_____

Visit/do next time: _____
_____
_____

Most memorable event: _____
_____
_____

Most fun things: _____
_____
_____
_____

Notes: _____
_____
_____
_____
_____
_____

Drawing or favorite photo:

Campground: _____ **Dates:** _____

Location:_____
Travel to Campground: *Miles:*_____ *Time:*_____ *Cost:*_____
Weather/Temperature:_____

Campground Information

Name:_____
Address:_____
Phone:_____
Site#:_____ Site for next time:_____
Cost:_____ $ ☐ Day ☐ Week ☐ Month
GPS:_____
Rating: ★☆☆☆☆☆☆☆☆☆
Water pressure ★☆☆☆☆ Location ★☆☆☆☆
Cleanliness   ★☆☆☆☆ Site size ★☆☆☆☆
Restrooms   ★☆☆☆☆ Noise   ★☆☆☆☆

Amenities:
☐ easy access   ☐ back-in   ☐ pull-through
☐ water   ☐ pet friendly ☐ laundry
☐ paved   ☐ sewer   ☐ electricity
☐ 15 amp   ☐ 30 amp   ☐ 50 amp
☐ shade   ☐ pool   ☐ restrooms
☐ store   ☐ picnic table ☐ fire ring
☐ firewood   ☐ tv   ☐ wifi
☐ security   ☐ ice   ☐ cafe

Activities:
☐ fishing   ☐ hiking   ☐ canoeing
☐ lake   ☐ river   ☐ hot tub
☐ fitness   ☐ bike   ☐ boat
☐ shuffleboard ☐ pickleball   ☐ golf

Camped with:_____
_____
_____

People met:_____
_____

New friends:_____
_____

Places visited:_____
_____
_____

Visit/do next time:_____
_____
_____

Most memorable event:

Most fun things:

Notes:

Drawing or favorite photo:

Campground: _____ **Dates:** _____

Location: _____

Travel to Campground: *Miles:* _____ *Time:* _____ *Cost:* _____

Weather/Temperature: _____

Campground Information

Name: _____

Address: _____

Phone: _____

Site#: _____ Site for next time: _____

Cost: _____ $ ☐ Day ☐ Week ☐ Month

GPS: _____

Rating: ★☆☆☆☆☆☆☆☆☆

Water pressure ★☆☆☆☆   Location ★☆☆☆☆

Cleanliness   ★☆☆☆☆   Site size ★☆☆☆☆

Restrooms   ★☆☆☆☆   Noise   ★☆☆☆☆

Amenities:
- ☐ easy access ☐ back-in   ☐ pull-through
- ☐ water   ☐ pet friendly ☐ laundry
- ☐ paved   ☐ sewer   ☐ electricity
- ☐ 15 amp   ☐ 30 amp   ☐ 50 amp
- ☐ shade   ☐ pool   ☐ restrooms
- ☐ store   ☐ picnic table ☐ fire ring
- ☐ firewood   ☐ tv   ☐ wifi
- ☐ security   ☐ ice   ☐ cafe

Activities:
- ☐ fishing   ☐ hiking   ☐ canoeing
- ☐ lake   ☐ river   ☐ hot tub
- ☐ fitness   ☐ bike   ☐ boat
- ☐ shuffleboard ☐ pickleball ☐ golf

Camped with: _____
_____
_____

People met: _____
_____

New friends: _____
_____

Places visited: _____
_____
_____

Visit/do next time: _____
_____
_____

Most memorable event:_____
_____
_____

Most fun things:_____
_____
_____
_____

Notes:_____
_____
_____
_____
_____
_____

Drawing or favorite photo:

Campground: _____   **Dates:** _____

Location:_____
Travel to Campground: *Miles:*_____ *Time:*_____ *Cost:*_____
Weather/Temperature:_____

Campground Information

Name:_____
Address:_____
Phone:_____
Site#:_____ Site for next time:_____
Cost:_____ $ ☐ Day ☐ Week ☐ Month
GPS:_____
Rating: ★☆☆☆☆☆☆☆☆☆
Water pressure ★☆☆☆☆ Location ★☆☆☆☆
Cleanliness ★☆☆☆☆ Site size ★☆☆☆☆
Restrooms ★☆☆☆☆ Noise ★☆☆☆☆

Amenities:
☐ easy access ☐ back-in ☐ pull-through
☐ water ☐ pet friendly ☐ laundry
☐ paved ☐ sewer ☐ electricity
☐ 15 amp ☐ 30 amp ☐ 50 amp
☐ shade ☐ pool ☐ restrooms
☐ store ☐ picnic table ☐ fire ring
☐ firewood ☐ tv ☐ wifi
☐ security ☐ ice ☐ cafe

Activities:
☐ fishing ☐ hiking ☐ canoeing
☐ lake ☐ river ☐ hot tub
☐ fitness ☐ bike ☐ boat
☐ shuffleboard ☐ pickleball ☐ golf

Camped with:_____
_____
_____

People met:_____
_____

New friends:_____
_____

Places visited:_____
_____
_____

Visit/do next time:_____
_____
_____

Most memorable event:_____
_____
_____

Most fun things:_____
_____
_____
_____

Notes:_____
_____
_____
_____
_____
_____

Drawing or favorite photo:

Campground: _____ **Dates:** _____

Location: _____
Travel to Campground: *Miles:* _____ *Time:* _____ *Cost:* _____
Weather/Temperature: _____

Campground Information

Name: _____
Address: _____
Phone: _____
Site#: _____ Site for next time: _____
Cost: _____ $ ☐ Day ☐ Week ☐ Month
GPS: _____
Rating: ★☆☆☆☆☆☆☆☆☆
Water pressure ★☆☆☆☆ Location ★☆☆☆☆
Cleanliness   ★☆☆☆☆ Site size ★☆☆☆☆
Restrooms   ★☆☆☆☆ Noise   ★☆☆☆☆

Amenities:
☐ easy access   ☐ back-in   ☐ pull-through
☐ water   ☐ pet friendly   ☐ laundry
☐ paved   ☐ sewer   ☐ electricity
☐ 15 amp   ☐ 30 amp   ☐ 50 amp
☐ shade   ☐ pool   ☐ restrooms
☐ store   ☐ picnic table   ☐ fire ring
☐ firewood   ☐ tv   ☐ wifi
☐ security   ☐ ice   ☐ cafe

Activities:
☐ fishing   ☐ hiking   ☐ canoeing
☐ lake   ☐ river   ☐ hot tub
☐ fitness   ☐ bike   ☐ boat
☐ shuffleboard   ☐ pickleball   ☐ golf

Camped with: _____
_____
_____

People met: _____
_____

New friends: _____
_____

Places visited: _____
_____
_____

Visit/do next time: _____
_____
_____

Most memorable event:

Most fun things:

Notes:

Drawing or favorite photo:

Campground: _____ **Dates:** _____

Location: _____
Travel to Campground: *Miles:* _____ *Time:* _____ *Cost:* _____
Weather/Temperature: _____

Campground Information

Name: _____
Address: _____
Phone: _____
Site#: _____ Site for next time: _____
Cost: _____ $ ☐ Day ☐ Week ☐ Month
GPS: _____
Rating: ★☆☆☆☆☆☆☆☆☆
Water pressure ★☆☆☆☆ Location ★☆☆☆☆
Cleanliness   ★☆☆☆☆ Site size ★☆☆☆☆
Restrooms   ★☆☆☆☆ Noise   ★☆☆☆☆

Amenities:
- ☐ easy access ☐ back-in ☐ pull-through
- ☐ water ☐ pet friendly ☐ laundry
- ☐ paved ☐ sewer ☐ electricity
- ☐ 15 amp ☐ 30 amp ☐ 50 amp
- ☐ shade ☐ pool ☐ restrooms
- ☐ store ☐ picnic table ☐ fire ring
- ☐ firewood ☐ tv ☐ wifi
- ☐ security ☐ ice ☐ cafe

Activities:
- ☐ fishing ☐ hiking ☐ canoeing
- ☐ lake ☐ river ☐ hot tub
- ☐ fitness ☐ bike ☐ boat
- ☐ shuffleboard ☐ pickleball ☐ golf

Camped with: _____
_____
_____

People met: _____
_____

New friends: _____
_____

Places visited: _____
_____
_____

Visit/do next time: _____
_____
_____

Most memorable event: _____
_____
_____

Most fun things: _____
_____
_____
_____

Notes: _____
_____
_____
_____
_____

Drawing or favorite photo:

Campground: _____ **Dates:** _____

Location: _____

Travel to Campground: *Miles:* _____ *Time:* _____ *Cost:* _____

Weather/Temperature: _____

Campground Information

Name: _____

Address: _____

Phone: _____

Site#: _____ Site for next time: _____

Cost: _____ $ ☐ Day ☐ Week ☐ Month

GPS: _____

Rating: ★☆☆☆☆☆☆☆☆☆

Water pressure ★☆☆☆☆   Location ★☆☆☆☆

Cleanliness   ★☆☆☆☆   Site size ★☆☆☆☆

Restrooms   ★☆☆☆☆   Noise   ★☆☆☆☆

Amenities:
- ☐ easy access   ☐ back-in   ☐ pull-through
- ☐ water   ☐ pet friendly   ☐ laundry
- ☐ paved   ☐ sewer   ☐ electricity
- ☐ 15 amp   ☐ 30 amp   ☐ 50 amp
- ☐ shade   ☐ pool   ☐ restrooms
- ☐ store   ☐ picnic table   ☐ fire ring
- ☐ firewood   ☐ tv   ☐ wifi
- ☐ security   ☐ ice   ☐ cafe

Activities:
- ☐ fishing   ☐ hiking   ☐ canoeing
- ☐ lake   ☐ river   ☐ hot tub
- ☐ fitness   ☐ bike   ☐ boat
- ☐ shuffleboard   ☐ pickleball   ☐ golf

Camped with: _____
_____
_____

People met: _____
_____

New friends: _____
_____

Places visited: _____
_____
_____

Visit/do next time: _____
_____
_____

Most memorable event:_____
_____
_____

Most fun things:_____
_____
_____
_____

Notes:_____
_____
_____
_____
_____

Drawing or favorite photo:

Campground: _____ **Dates:** _____

Location: _____

Travel to Campground: *Miles:* _____ *Time:* _____ *Cost:* _____

Weather/Temperature: _____

Campground Information

Name: _____

Address: _____

Phone: _____

Site#: _____ Site for next time: _____

Cost: _____ $ ☐ Day ☐ Week ☐ Month

GPS: _____

Rating: ★☆☆☆☆☆☆☆☆☆

Water pressure ★☆☆☆☆ Location ★☆☆☆☆

Cleanliness ★☆☆☆☆ Site size ★☆☆☆☆

Restrooms ★☆☆☆☆ Noise ★☆☆☆☆

Amenities:
- ☐ easy access ☐ back-in ☐ pull-through
- ☐ water ☐ pet friendly ☐ laundry
- ☐ paved ☐ sewer ☐ electricity
- ☐ 15 amp ☐ 30 amp ☐ 50 amp
- ☐ shade ☐ pool ☐ restrooms
- ☐ store ☐ picnic table ☐ fire ring
- ☐ firewood ☐ tv ☐ wifi
- ☐ security ☐ ice ☐ cafe

Activities:
- ☐ fishing ☐ hiking ☐ canoeing
- ☐ lake ☐ river ☐ hot tub
- ☐ fitness ☐ bike ☐ boat
- ☐ shuffleboard ☐ pickleball ☐ golf

Camped with: _____
_____

People met: _____
_____

New friends: _____
_____

Places visited: _____
_____
_____

Visit/do next time: _____
_____
_____

Most memorable event: _____
_____
_____

Most fun things: _____
_____
_____
_____

Notes: _____
_____
_____
_____
_____
_____

Drawing or favorite photo:

Campground: _____ **Dates:** _____

Location: _____

Travel to Campground: *Miles:* _____ *Time:* _____ *Cost:* _____

Weather/Temperature: _____

Campground Information

Name: _____

Address: _____

Phone: _____

Site#: _____ Site for next time: _____

Cost: _____ $ ☐ Day ☐ Week ☐ Month

GPS: _____

Rating: ★☆☆☆☆☆☆☆☆☆

Water pressure ★☆☆☆☆   Location ★☆☆☆☆
Cleanliness   ★☆☆☆☆   Site size ★☆☆☆☆
Restrooms   ★☆☆☆☆   Noise   ★☆☆☆☆

Amenities:
- ☐ easy access   ☐ back-in   ☐ pull-through
- ☐ water   ☐ pet friendly ☐ laundry
- ☐ paved   ☐ sewer   ☐ electricity
- ☐ 15 amp   ☐ 30 amp   ☐ 50 amp
- ☐ shade   ☐ pool   ☐ restrooms
- ☐ store   ☐ picnic table ☐ fire ring
- ☐ firewood   ☐ tv   ☐ wifi
- ☐ security   ☐ ice   ☐ cafe

Activities:
- ☐ fishing   ☐ hiking   ☐ canoeing
- ☐ lake   ☐ river   ☐ hot tub
- ☐ fitness   ☐ bike   ☐ boat
- ☐ shuffleboard   ☐ pickleball   ☐ golf

Camped with: _____
_____
_____

People met: _____
_____

New friends: _____
_____

Places visited: _____
_____
_____

Visit/do next time: _____
_____
_____

Most memorable event: _____
_____
_____

Most fun things: _____
_____
_____
_____
_____

Notes: _____
_____
_____
_____
_____
_____

Drawing or favorite photo:

Campground: _____ **Dates:** _____

Location: _____
Travel to Campground: *Miles:* _____ *Time:* _____ *Cost:* _____
Weather/Temperature: _____

Campground Information

Name: _____
Address: _____
Phone: _____
Site#: _____ Site for next time: _____
Cost: _____ $ ☐ Day ☐ Week ☐ Month
GPS: _____
Rating: ★☆☆☆☆☆☆☆☆☆
Water pressure ★☆☆☆☆   Location ★☆☆☆☆
Cleanliness   ★☆☆☆☆   Site size ★☆☆☆☆
Restrooms   ★☆☆☆☆   Noise   ★☆☆☆☆

Amenities:
☐ easy access   ☐ back-in   ☐ pull-through
☐ water   ☐ pet friendly ☐ laundry
☐ paved   ☐ sewer   ☐ electricity
☐ 15 amp   ☐ 30 amp   ☐ 50 amp
☐ shade   ☐ pool   ☐ restrooms
☐ store   ☐ picnic table ☐ fire ring
☐ firewood   ☐ tv   ☐ wifi
☐ security   ☐ ice   ☐ cafe

Activities:
☐ fishing   ☐ hiking   ☐ canoeing
☐ lake   ☐ river   ☐ hot tub
☐ fitness   ☐ bike   ☐ boat
☐ shuffleboard   ☐ pickleball   ☐ golf

Camped with: _____
_____
_____

People met: _____
_____

New friends: _____
_____

Places visited: _____
_____
_____

Visit/do next time: _____
_____
_____

Most memorable event:_____
_____
_____

Most fun things:_____
_____
_____
_____

Notes:_____
_____
_____
_____
_____
_____

Drawing or favorite photo:

Campground: _____ **Dates:** _____

Location: _____
Travel to Campground: *Miles:* _____ *Time:* _____ *Cost:* _____
Weather/Temperature: _____

Campground Information

Name: _____
Address: _____
Phone: _____
Site#: _____ Site for next time: _____
Cost: _____ $ ☐ Day ☐ Week ☐ Month
GPS: _____

Rating: ★☆☆☆☆☆☆☆☆☆
Water pressure ★☆☆☆☆ Location ★☆☆☆☆
Cleanliness   ★☆☆☆☆ Site size ★☆☆☆☆
Restrooms   ★☆☆☆☆ Noise   ★☆☆☆☆

Amenities:
☐ easy access   ☐ back-in   ☐ pull-through
☐ water   ☐ pet friendly ☐ laundry
☐ paved   ☐ sewer   ☐ electricity
☐ 15 amp   ☐ 30 amp   ☐ 50 amp
☐ shade   ☐ pool   ☐ restrooms
☐ store   ☐ picnic table ☐ fire ring
☐ firewood   ☐ tv   ☐ wifi
☐ security   ☐ ice   ☐ cafe

Activities:
☐ fishing   ☐ hiking   ☐ canoeing
☐ lake   ☐ river   ☐ hot tub
☐ fitness   ☐ bike   ☐ boat
☐ shuffleboard ☐ pickleball   ☐ golf

Camped with: _____
_____
_____

People met: _____
_____

New friends: _____
_____

Places visited: _____
_____
_____

Visit/do next time: _____
_____
_____

Most memorable event:_____
_____
_____

Most fun things:_____
_____
_____
_____

Notes:_____
_____
_____
_____
_____
_____

Drawing or favorite photo:

Campground: _____ Dates: _____

Location: _____
Travel to Campground: *Miles:* _____ *Time:* _____ *Cost:* _____
Weather/Temperature: _____

Campground Information

Name: _____
Address: _____
Phone: _____
Site#: _____ Site for next time: _____
Cost: _____ $ ☐ Day ☐ Week ☐ Month
GPS: _____
Rating: ★☆☆☆☆☆☆☆☆☆
Water pressure ★☆☆☆☆ Location ★☆☆☆☆
Cleanliness   ★☆☆☆☆ Site size ★☆☆☆☆
Restrooms   ★☆☆☆☆ Noise   ★☆☆☆☆

Amenities:
☐ easy access   ☐ back-in   ☐ pull-through
☐ water   ☐ pet friendly   ☐ laundry
☐ paved   ☐ sewer   ☐ electricity
☐ 15 amp   ☐ 30 amp   ☐ 50 amp
☐ shade   ☐ pool   ☐ restrooms
☐ store   ☐ picnic table   ☐ fire ring
☐ firewood   ☐ tv   ☐ wifi
☐ security   ☐ ice   ☐ cafe

Activities:
☐ fishing   ☐ hiking   ☐ canoeing
☐ lake   ☐ river   ☐ hot tub
☐ fitness   ☐ bike   ☐ boat
☐ shuffleboard ☐ pickleball   ☐ golf

Camped with: _____
_____
_____

People met: _____
_____

New friends: _____
_____

Places visited: _____
_____
_____

Visit/do next time: _____
_____
_____

Most memorable event:

Most fun things:

Notes:

Drawing or favorite photo:

Campground: _____ **Dates:** _____

Location: _____
Travel to Campground: *Miles:* _____ *Time:* _____ *Cost:* _____
Weather/Temperature: _____

Campground Information

Name: _____
Address: _____
Phone: _____
Site#: _____ Site for next time: _____
Cost: _____ $ ☐ Day ☐ Week ☐ Month
GPS: _____
Rating: ★☆☆☆☆☆☆☆☆☆
Water pressure ★☆☆☆☆ Location ★☆☆☆☆
Cleanliness   ★☆☆☆☆ Site size ★☆☆☆☆
Restrooms   ★☆☆☆☆ Noise   ★☆☆☆☆

Amenities:
☐ easy access   ☐ back-in   ☐ pull-through
☐ water   ☐ pet friendly ☐ laundry
☐ paved   ☐ sewer   ☐ electricity
☐ 15 amp   ☐ 30 amp   ☐ 50 amp
☐ shade   ☐ pool   ☐ restrooms
☐ store   ☐ picnic table ☐ fire ring
☐ firewood   ☐ tv   ☐ wifi
☐ security   ☐ ice   ☐ cafe

Activities:
☐ fishing   ☐ hiking   ☐ canoeing
☐ lake   ☐ river   ☐ hot tub
☐ fitness   ☐ bike   ☐ boat
☐ shuffleboard   ☐ pickleball   ☐ golf

Camped with: _____
_____
_____

People met: _____
_____

New friends: _____
_____

Places visited: _____
_____
_____

Visit/do next time: _____
_____
_____

Most memorable event:_____
_____
_____

Most fun things:_____
_____
_____
_____

Notes:_____
_____
_____
_____
_____

Drawing or favorite photo:

Campground: _____ **Dates:** _____

Location: _____
Travel to Campground: *Miles:* _____ *Time:* _____ *Cost:* _____
Weather/Temperature: _____

Campground Information

Name: _____
Address: _____
Phone: _____
Site#: _____ Site for next time: _____
Cost: _____ $ ☐ Day ☐ Week ☐ Month
GPS: _____
Rating: ★☆☆☆☆☆☆☆☆☆
Water pressure ★☆☆☆☆   Location ★☆☆☆☆
Cleanliness   ★☆☆☆☆   Site size ★☆☆☆☆
Restrooms   ★☆☆☆☆   Noise   ★☆☆☆☆

Amenities:
☐ easy access   ☐ back-in   ☐ pull-through
☐ water   ☐ pet friendly   ☐ laundry
☐ paved   ☐ sewer   ☐ electricity
☐ 15 amp   ☐ 30 amp   ☐ 50 amp
☐ shade   ☐ pool   ☐ restrooms
☐ store   ☐ picnic table   ☐ fire ring
☐ firewood   ☐ tv   ☐ wifi
☐ security   ☐ ice   ☐ cafe

Activities:
☐ fishing   ☐ hiking   ☐ canoeing
☐ lake   ☐ river   ☐ hot tub
☐ fitness   ☐ bike   ☐ boat
☐ shuffleboard   ☐ pickleball   ☐ golf

Camped with: _____
_____
_____

People met: _____
_____

New friends: _____
_____

Places visited: _____
_____
_____

Visit/do next time: _____
_____
_____

Most memorable event:_____
_____
_____

Most fun things:_____
_____
_____
_____
_____

Notes:_____
_____
_____
_____
_____
_____

Drawing or favorite photo:

Campground: _____ **Dates:** _____

Location: _____
Travel to Campground: *Miles:* _____ *Time:* _____ *Cost:* _____
Weather/Temperature: _____

Campground Information

Name: _____
Address: _____
Phone: _____
Site#: _____ Site for next time: _____
Cost: _____ $ ☐ Day ☐ Week ☐ Month
GPS: _____
Rating: ★☆☆☆☆☆☆☆☆☆
Water pressure ★☆☆☆☆ Location ★☆☆☆☆
Cleanliness ★☆☆☆☆ Site size ★☆☆☆☆
Restrooms ★☆☆☆☆ Noise ★☆☆☆☆

Amenities:
- ☐ easy access ☐ back-in ☐ pull-through
- ☐ water ☐ pet friendly ☐ laundry
- ☐ paved ☐ sewer ☐ electricity
- ☐ 15 amp ☐ 30 amp ☐ 50 amp
- ☐ shade ☐ pool ☐ restrooms
- ☐ store ☐ picnic table ☐ fire ring
- ☐ firewood ☐ tv ☐ wifi
- ☐ security ☐ ice ☐ cafe

Activities:
- ☐ fishing ☐ hiking ☐ canoeing
- ☐ lake ☐ river ☐ hot tub
- ☐ fitness ☐ bike ☐ boat
- ☐ shuffleboard ☐ pickleball ☐ golf

Camped with: _____
_____
_____

People met: _____
_____

New friends: _____
_____

Places visited: _____
_____
_____

Visit/do next time: _____
_____
_____

Most memorable event:_____
_____
_____

Most fun things:_____
_____
_____
_____

Notes:_____
_____
_____
_____
_____

Drawing or favorite photo:

Campground: _____ **Dates:** _____

Location:_____

Travel to Campground: *Miles:*_____ *Time:*_____ *Cost:*_____

Weather/Temperature:_____

Campground Information

Name:_____

Address:_____

Phone:_____

Site#:_____ Site for next time:_____

Cost:_____ $ ☐ Day ☐ Week ☐ Month

GPS: _____

Rating: ★☆☆☆☆☆☆☆☆☆

Water pressure ★☆☆☆☆ Location ★☆☆☆☆

Cleanliness ★☆☆☆☆ Site size ★☆☆☆☆

Restrooms ★☆☆☆☆ Noise ★☆☆☆☆

Amenities:
- ☐ easy access ☐ back-in ☐ pull-through
- ☐ water ☐ pet friendly ☐ laundry
- ☐ paved ☐ sewer ☐ electricity
- ☐ 15 amp ☐ 30 amp ☐ 50 amp
- ☐ shade ☐ pool ☐ restrooms
- ☐ store ☐ picnic table ☐ fire ring
- ☐ firewood ☐ tv ☐ wifi
- ☐ security ☐ ice ☐ cafe

Activities:
- ☐ fishing ☐ hiking ☐ canoeing
- ☐ lake ☐ river ☐ hot tub
- ☐ fitness ☐ bike ☐ boat
- ☐ shuffleboard ☐ pickleball ☐ golf

Camped with:_____
_____
_____

People met:_____
_____

New friends:_____
_____

Places visited:_____
_____
_____

Visit/do next time:_____
_____
_____

Most memorable event: _____
_____
_____

Most fun things: _____
_____
_____
_____

Notes: _____
_____
_____
_____
_____
_____

Drawing or favorite photo:

Campground: _____ **Dates:** _____

Location: _____
Travel to Campground: *Miles:* _____ *Time:* _____ *Cost:* _____
Weather/Temperature: _____

Campground Information

Name: _____
Address: _____
Phone: _____
Site#: _____ Site for next time: _____
Cost: _____ $ ☐ Day ☐ Week ☐ Month
GPS: _____
Rating: ★☆☆☆☆☆☆☆☆☆
Water pressure ★☆☆☆☆ Location ★☆☆☆☆
Cleanliness   ★☆☆☆☆ Site size ★☆☆☆☆
Restrooms   ★☆☆☆☆ Noise   ★☆☆☆☆

Amenities:
☐ easy access   ☐ back-in   ☐ pull-through
☐ water   ☐ pet friendly   ☐ laundry
☐ paved   ☐ sewer   ☐ electricity
☐ 15 amp   ☐ 30 amp   ☐ 50 amp
☐ shade   ☐ pool   ☐ restrooms
☐ store   ☐ picnic table   ☐ fire ring
☐ firewood   ☐ tv   ☐ wifi
☐ security   ☐ ice   ☐ cafe

Activities:
☐ fishing   ☐ hiking   ☐ canoeing
☐ lake   ☐ river   ☐ hot tub
☐ fitness   ☐ bike   ☐ boat
☐ shuffleboard ☐ pickleball   ☐ golf

Camped with: _____
_____
_____

People met: _____
_____
_____

New friends: _____
_____
_____

Places visited: _____
_____
_____

Visit/do next time: _____
_____
_____

Most memorable event:_____
_____
_____

Most fun things:_____
_____
_____
_____

Notes:_____
_____
_____
_____
_____
_____

Drawing or favorite photo:

Campground: _____ **Dates:** _____

Location: _____
Travel to Campground: *Miles:* _____ *Time:* _____ *Cost:* _____
Weather/Temperature: _____

Campground Information

Name: _____
Address: _____
Phone: _____
Site#: _____ Site for next time: _____
Cost: _____ $ ☐ Day ☐ Week ☐ Month
GPS: _____
Rating: ★☆☆☆☆☆☆☆☆☆
Water pressure ★☆☆☆☆   Location ★☆☆☆☆
Cleanliness   ★☆☆☆☆   Site size ★☆☆☆☆
Restrooms   ★☆☆☆☆   Noise   ★☆☆☆☆

Amenities:
☐ easy access   ☐ back-in   ☐ pull-through
☐ water   ☐ pet friendly ☐ laundry
☐ paved   ☐ sewer   ☐ electricity
☐ 15 amp   ☐ 30 amp   ☐ 50 amp
☐ shade   ☐ pool   ☐ restrooms
☐ store   ☐ picnic table ☐ fire ring
☐ firewood   ☐ tv   ☐ wifi
☐ security   ☐ ice   ☐ cafe

Activities:
☐ fishing   ☐ hiking   ☐ canoeing
☐ lake   ☐ river   ☐ hot tub
☐ fitness   ☐ bike   ☐ boat
☐ shuffleboard ☐ pickleball   ☐ golf

Camped with: _____
_____

People met: _____
_____

New friends: _____
_____

Places visited: _____
_____
_____

Visit/do next time: _____
_____
_____

Most memorable event:_____
_____
_____

Most fun things:_____
_____
_____
_____

Notes:_____
_____
_____
_____
_____
_____

Drawing or favorite photo:

Campground: _____ **Dates:** _____

Location: _____

Travel to Campground: *Miles:* _____ *Time:* _____ *Cost:* _____

Weather/Temperature: _____

Campground Information

Name: _____

Address: _____

Phone: _____

Site#: _____ Site for next time: _____

Cost: _____ $ ☐ Day ☐ Week ☐ Month

GPS: _____

Rating: ★☆☆☆☆☆☆☆☆☆

Water pressure ★☆☆☆☆ Location ★☆☆☆☆

Cleanliness ★☆☆☆☆ Site size ★☆☆☆☆

Restrooms   ★☆☆☆☆ Noise   ★☆☆☆☆

Amenities:
- ☐ easy access ☐ back-in ☐ pull-through
- ☐ water ☐ pet friendly ☐ laundry
- ☐ paved ☐ sewer ☐ electricity
- ☐ 15 amp ☐ 30 amp ☐ 50 amp
- ☐ shade ☐ pool ☐ restrooms
- ☐ store ☐ picnic table ☐ fire ring
- ☐ firewood ☐ tv ☐ wifi
- ☐ security ☐ ice ☐ cafe

Activities:
- ☐ fishing ☐ hiking ☐ canoeing
- ☐ lake ☐ river ☐ hot tub
- ☐ fitness ☐ bike ☐ boat
- ☐ shuffleboard ☐ pickleball ☐ golf

Camped with: _____
_____
_____

People met: _____
_____

New friends: _____
_____

Places visited: _____
_____
_____

Visit/do next time: _____
_____
_____

Most memorable event: _____
_____
_____

Most fun things: _____
_____
_____
_____

Notes: _____
_____
_____
_____
_____
_____

Drawing or favorite photo:

Campground: _____ Dates: _____

Location: _____
Travel to Campground: *Miles:* _____ *Time:* _____ *Cost:* _____
Weather/Temperature: _____

Campground Information

Name: _____
Address: _____
Phone: _____
Site#: _____ Site for next time: _____
Cost: _____ $ ☐ Day ☐ Week ☐ Month
GPS: _____
Rating: ★☆☆☆☆☆☆☆☆☆
Water pressure ★☆☆☆☆ Location ★☆☆☆☆
Cleanliness   ★☆☆☆☆ Site size ★☆☆☆☆
Restrooms   ★☆☆☆☆ Noise   ★☆☆☆☆

Amenities:
☐ easy access   ☐ back-in   ☐ pull-through
☐ water   ☐ pet friendly   ☐ laundry
☐ paved   ☐ sewer   ☐ electricity
☐ 15 amp   ☐ 30 amp   ☐ 50 amp
☐ shade   ☐ pool   ☐ restrooms
☐ store   ☐ picnic table   ☐ fire ring
☐ firewood   ☐ tv   ☐ wifi
☐ security   ☐ ice   ☐ cafe

Activities:
☐ fishing   ☐ hiking   ☐ canoeing
☐ lake   ☐ river   ☐ hot tub
☐ fitness   ☐ bike   ☐ boat
☐ shuffleboard   ☐ pickleball   ☐ golf

Camped with: _____
_____
_____

People met: _____
_____

New friends: _____
_____

Places visited: _____
_____
_____

Visit/do next time: _____
_____
_____

Most memorable event: _____
_____
_____

Most fun things: _____
_____
_____
_____

Notes: _____
_____
_____
_____
_____
_____

Drawing or favorite photo:

Campground: _____ **Dates:** _____

Location:_____

Travel to Campground: *Miles:*_____ *Time:*_____ *Cost:*_____

Weather/Temperature:_____

Campground Information

Name:_____

Address:_____

Phone:_____

Site#:_____ Site for next time:_____

Cost:_____ $ ☐ Day ☐ Week ☐ Month

GPS:_____

Rating: ★☆☆☆☆☆☆☆☆☆

Water pressure ★☆☆☆☆ Location ★☆☆☆☆

Cleanliness ★☆☆☆☆ Site size ★☆☆☆☆

Restrooms ★☆☆☆☆ Noise ★☆☆☆☆

Amenities:
- ☐ easy access ☐ back-in ☐ pull-through
- ☐ water ☐ pet friendly ☐ laundry
- ☐ paved ☐ sewer ☐ electricity
- ☐ 15 amp ☐ 30 amp ☐ 50 amp
- ☐ shade ☐ pool ☐ restrooms
- ☐ store ☐ picnic table ☐ fire ring
- ☐ firewood ☐ tv ☐ wifi
- ☐ security ☐ ice ☐ cafe

Activities:
- ☐ fishing ☐ hiking ☐ canoeing
- ☐ lake ☐ river ☐ hot tub
- ☐ fitness ☐ bike ☐ boat
- ☐ shuffleboard ☐ pickleball ☐ golf

Camped with:_____
_____
_____

People met:_____
_____

New friends:_____
_____

Places visited:_____
_____
_____

Visit/do next time:_____
_____
_____

Most memorable event:

Most fun things:

Notes:

Drawing or favorite photo:

Campground: _____ **Dates:** _____

Location: _____

Travel to Campground: *Miles:* _____   *Time:* _____   *Cost:* _____

Weather/Temperature: _____

Campground Information

Name: _____

Address: _____

Phone: _____

Site#: _____   Site for next time: _____

Cost: _____ $ ☐ Day ☐ Week ☐ Month

GPS: _____

Rating: ★☆☆☆☆☆☆☆☆☆

Water pressure ★☆☆☆☆   Location ★☆☆☆☆

Cleanliness ★☆☆☆☆   Site size ★☆☆☆☆

Restrooms ★☆☆☆☆   Noise ★☆☆☆☆

Amenities:
- ☐ easy access   ☐ back-in   ☐ pull-through
- ☐ water   ☐ pet friendly   ☐ laundry
- ☐ paved   ☐ sewer   ☐ electricity
- ☐ 15 amp   ☐ 30 amp   ☐ 50 amp
- ☐ shade   ☐ pool   ☐ restrooms
- ☐ store   ☐ picnic table   ☐ fire ring
- ☐ firewood   ☐ tv   ☐ wifi
- ☐ security   ☐ ice   ☐ cafe

Activities:
- ☐ fishing   ☐ hiking   ☐ canoeing
- ☐ lake   ☐ river   ☐ hot tub
- ☐ fitness   ☐ bike   ☐ boat
- ☐ shuffleboard   ☐ pickleball   ☐ golf

Camped with: _____
_____
_____

People met: _____
_____

New friends: _____
_____

Places visited: _____
_____
_____

Visit/do next time: _____
_____
_____

Manufactured by Amazon.ca
Bolton, ON